The Great Songs of Michael Jackson.

THIS PUBLICATION IS NOT AUTHORISED
FOR SALE IN THE UNITED STATES
OF AMERICA AND/OR CANADA.

Exclusive Distributors:
Music Sales Limited,
8/9 Frith Street, London W1V 5TZ, England.
Music Sales Pty. Limited,
120 Rothschild Avenue, Rosebery, NSW 2018, Australia.

This book © Copyright 1984 by Wise Publications
UK ISBN 0.7119.0483.9
UK Order No. AM36401

Book designed by Pearce Marchbank Studio.
Cover photographs by Photofeatures.
Compiled by Peter Evans.

*Music Sales complete catalogue lists thousands of titles and is free
from your local music book shop, or direct from Music Sales Limited.
Please send a cheque/postal order for £1.50 for postage to:
Music Sales Limited, Newmarket Road, Bury St. Edmunds, Suffolk IP33 3YB.*

*Printed in England by
Halstan & Co. Limited, Amersham, Bucks.*

Wise Publications
London/New York/Sydney

Ben.

Words: Don Black
Music: Walter Scharf

Rockin' Robin.

Words & Music: Jimmie Thomas

Bright Rock tempo

VERSE

1-3 He rocks in the tree tops, all the day long, Hop-pin'and a bop-pin'and a sing-in' his song.
2 Ev'ry lit-tle swal-low, ev'ry chick-a-dee, Ev'ry lit-tle bird in the tall oak tree. The

All the lit-tle birds on Jay-bird street, love to hear the ro-bin go "Tweet, tweet, tweet."
wise old owl, the big black crow, flap their wings, sing-in' "Go bird, go."

CHORUS

Rock-in' Ro-bin, Rock-in' Ro-bin,

Blow, Rock-in' Ro-bin, 'cause we're real-ly gon-na rock to night.

PATTER

pret-ty lit-tle ra-ven at the bird band-stand, taught him how to do the bop and it was grand. They

start-ed go-in' stead-y, and bless my soul, He out-bopped the buz-zard and the o-ri-ole. He

Got To Be There.

Words & Music: Elliot Willensky

loves me._____ 'Cause when I look in {her/his} eyes,___ I__

_____ re-al-ize I need {her/him} shar - ing the world__ be - side

me._____ { So, I've got to be there,__got to be there_____ in the morn - / That's why I've got to be there,__got to be there_____ where love__

____ ing, and wel-come {her/him} in - to my world,_____ and / __ be - gins and that's ev - 'ry-where {she/he} goes; _____ I've

One Day In Your Life.

Words: Renee Armand
Music: Samuel F. Brown III

She's Out Of My Life.

Words & Music: Tom Bahler

Rock With You.

Words & Music: Rod Temperton

Moderate Tempo Rock

Girl,   close your eyes,   let that   rhy-thm get in - to
Out on   the floor,___   there ain't   no - bod-y there   but

you.   Don't   try   to fight _____ it,   there ain't
us.   Girl, _____ when you   dance,   there's a

Baby Be Mine.

Words & Music: Rod Temperton

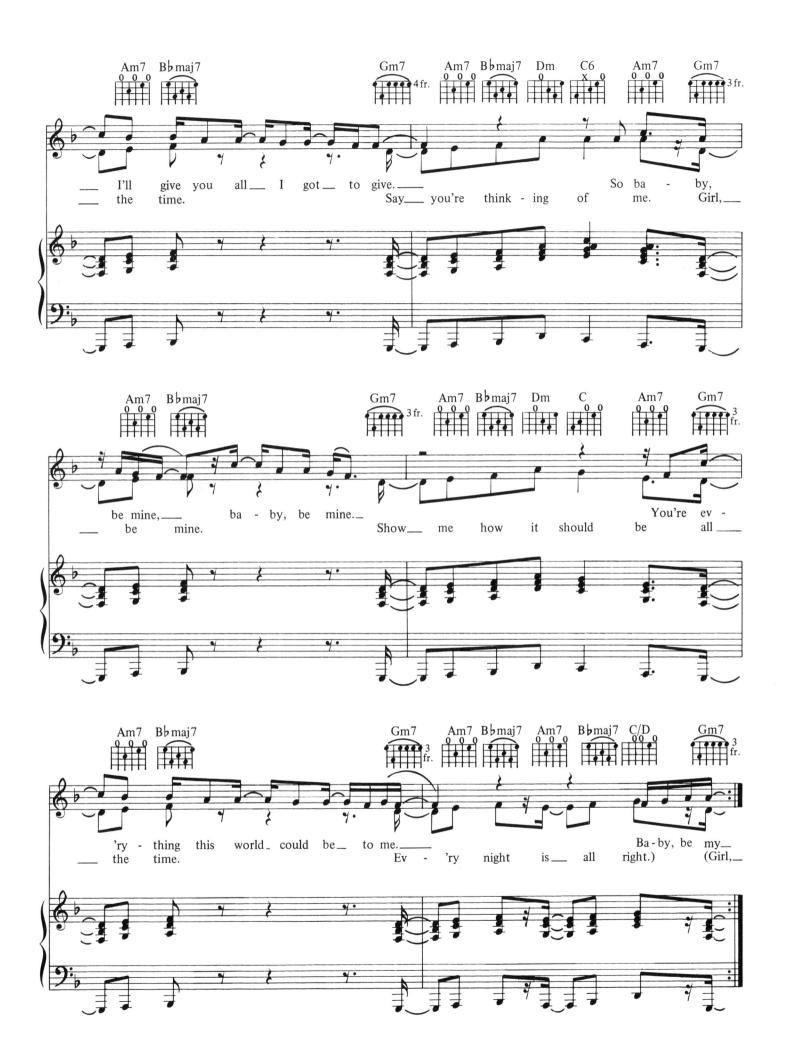

The Lady In My Life.

Words & Music: Rod Temperton

Moderately slow, in 2

You're ev-'ry won-der in this world to me, a treas-ure time won't steal a - way.

So lis-ten to my heart. Lay your bod-y close to mine.

And I will keep you warm through the shad-ows of the night.

beat of ec - sta - sy._____ Come to me._____

D. S. % al Coda ⊕   *Coda*

Repeat (vocal al lib) and fade

Thriller.

Words & Music: Rod Temperton

Moderately bright

It's close to mid - night,___ and some-thin' e - vil's lurk - in' in the dark.
You hear the door___ slam___ and re - al - ize there's no-where left to run.
They're out to get___ you.___ There's de - mons clos - in' in on ev - 'ry side.___

RAP: Darkness falls across the land.
      The midnight hour is close at hand.
      Creatures crawl in search of blood
      To terrorize y'awl's neighborhood.
      And whosoever shall be found
      Without the soul for getting down
      Must stand and face the hounds of hell
      And rot inside a corpse's shell.

      The foulest stench is in the air,
      The funk of forty thousand years,
      And grizzly ghouls from every tomb
      Are closing in to seal your doom.
      And though you fight to stay alive,
      Your body starts to shiver,
      For no mere mortal can resist
      The evil of a thriller.

Off The Wall.

Words & Music: Rod Temperton

1. When the

world is on your shoul - der ——— Got - ta straight-en up your act and boo - gie
shout out all you want to ——— 'Cos there ain't no sin in folks all get-ting

down ——— If you can't hang with the feel - in' ——— Then there
loud ——— If you take the chance to do it ——— Then there

ain't no room for you in this part of town _____ 'Cos we're the par___ ty peo-ple
ain't no one who's gon - na put you down _____

night and day, ___ Liv - in' cra___ zy, that's the on - ly way. ___ So ___ to - night _____ Got to

leave that nine to five up- on the shelf And just en - joy your-self. ___

Groove _____ and let the mad-ness in the mu - sic get to you. ___ Life ain't so

bad at all, ___ all _____ If you live it off the wall. Life ain't so bad at

see an ex - hi - bi - tion? ——— Bet-ter do it now be-fore you get too

old. ——— 'Cos we're the par —— ty peo-ple night and day, ———

'Liv - in' cra - zy, that's the on - ly way. So —— to - night ——— Got to

leave that nine to five up-on the shelf And just en - joy your-self. ——

Groove ——— and let the mad-ness in the mu - sic get to you. ——— Life ain't so